Breaking the Silence

Healing and Recovery for Date Rape Survivors

Marga Hogenhuis-Flokstra

Table Of Contents

Chapter 1: The Case

Broken and Torn

At my practice, a young woman aged 21 comes to see me. Right on time, she arrives at my doorstep. She almost disappears under her big coat, big scarf and her long brown hair. Unaccustomed, she walks on and I point her to the chairs we can sit on. I ask her what she wants to drink. Tea she would like. When I sit opposite her, having given her tea, I can observe her.

She is visibly nervous and fidgets a lot with her clothes. She looks tired. Her hair is messy and her face looks pale, which is further emphasised by all the black she is wearing. The tights she is wearing are broken. It has a large hole and a ladder that has already progressed quite a bit both ways. The shirt she is wearing has stains all over it. The big heavy black Dr Martens are completely torn in half at the back. Nothing is whole or clean. She comes across as somewhat untidy and unkempt as a result.

Symbolically, it tells me that she is "broken and torn" and considers herself dirty. By the way, this is my interpretation and does not rest on facts or any truth. Still, it helps me to look at the symbolism. I also often ask if it is correct. And often it is correct.

I ask her what brought her to my practice. Of course, I had already understood the reason from the application email, but still I ask about it so she can tell me in her own words. And then she starts talking...

She tells me that last year, after an evening at the pub, she woke up 14 hours later in a hotel room, completely naked and with no memory of how she got there or with whom...

This as an introduction to this research. A research I did as an assignment for my course in which I get to describe and present a case study. The assignment was to choose a case that I could learn the most from. Or to take a topic about which not much is known yet.

So little can be found on this subject that I decided to publish this little research in book form. I hope this will bring more knowledge into the world so that a lot of people can benefit from it. Not only therapists but also victims. So that they know they are not alone and that there is help.

Because I think it's important that you, the reader, get a feel for this case, I chose this way to write. It is not just a nameless client or case, she is a human being and a beautiful young woman.

And so there is trauma, trauma without her knowing what happened....

Page 5

Fear does not change yesterday's sorrow

or solve tomorrow's problems.

- Corrie ten Boom

Chapter 2: The Client

All the attention always went to my sister.

There is something wrong with her and I obviously didn't need attention.

She is young, just 21 years old. She studied and after studying Music, she started travelling and did a silence retreat in India, among other things. Then she trained as a Yoga instructor, NLP practitioner and she is now training to become an NLP Master.

She grew up bilingual in the Netherlands. Her father is Dutch and her mother English. Her father is an entrepreneur and owns a pub somewhere in a capital city. She currently lives above this pub and occasionally works behind the bar. She has two older sisters.

As an adolescent, she had a period when she felt depressed and cut herself (self-mutilation). From what she told me, I drew the conclusion that this stemmed from too low self-esteem. She had continually felt like she was in 2nd place. Or maybe even 3rd place or last place....

This probably originated in her early years. It all has to do with her eldest sister. This sister required quite a bit of extra attention throughout her childhood. What exactly was going on I haven't asked (yet). But what she told me was that her sister was not quite keeping up, apparently because there was something wrong in her development.

My client is the youngest of three children.

Chapter 3: The Research Question

With the help of this case study, I wanted to learn more about the effects of a date-rape involving drug use.

The questions I asked myself during this research:

What are the psychological and (psycho)somatic symptoms associated with this particular trauma?

What interventions can I apply?

As a therapist, how do you deal with the fact that there are almost no memories?

What can you offer to your client?

What can you do?

What is better not to do?

Can I read about it?

My intention was to gain more insight so that I can give my client the best help I can.

All drugs are a waste of time. They destroy your memory and your self-respect

and everything that goes along with your self-esteem.

- Kurt Corbain

Chapter 4: Which drugs are used?

Effects and side effects

Mainly two types of drugs are described that are associated with date-rape. Namely GHB and Rohypnol. Both types are basically intended as sedatives. Of course, depending on the doses and for most people (It can vary from person to person. Some can also make uncontrollable movements from it).

In this case study, I will therefore only discuss these two types. GHB and Rohypnol both act on the neurotransmitters GABA. GABA is abundant in the brain, pre- already in synaptic transmissions, in the grey matter of the brain and in the nigrostriatal system. GABA helps balance brain functioning. It helps prevent outliers in every imaginable area by slowing down in time. As a result, GABA facilitates the basic sense of security.

These GABA neurotransmitters have an inhibitory function. Neurotransmitters enable communication between neurons via messenger substances.

GABA is a non-essential amino acid. There are stimulating (exiting) and inhibiting (inhibiting) neurotransmitters and the two keep each other in balance. When there is over-activity in neurons, GABA that has an inhibitory activity will inhibit this over-activity. As a result, GABA acts as a natural tranquilliser, inhibits nerve impulses and has stress-regulating activity.

GABA (as a medicine) is used to reduce anxiety, improve mood, reduce Pre Menstrual Syndrome (PMS) and in treating ADHD. GABA is also used in other neuropsychiatric conditions such as stress, epilepsy and sleep disorders. It is also used for muscle building, fat burning, Stabilizing blood pressure and reducing pain.

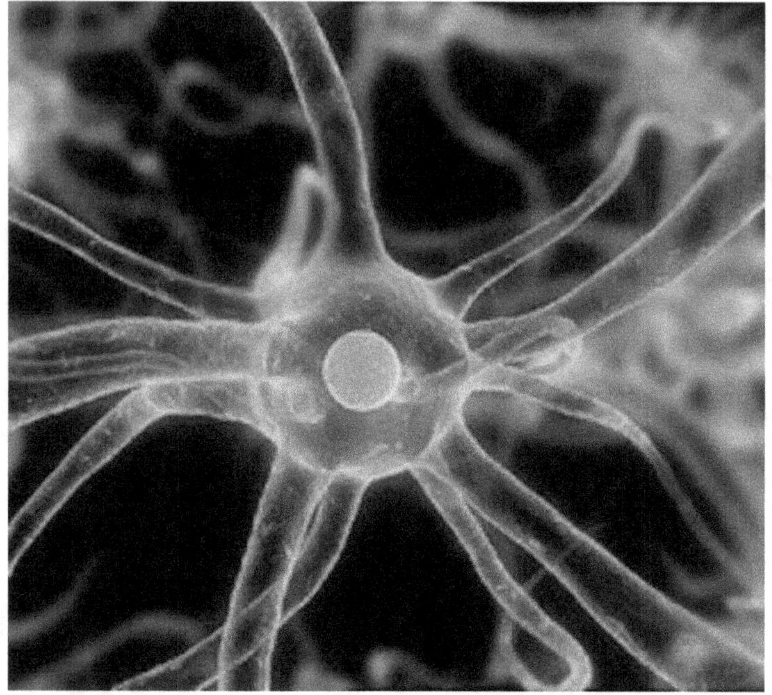

What is GHB?

GHB is short for gamma-hydroxybutyric acid. This substance, even if you do not use it, is present in very small quantities in your body. In the 1960s and 1970s, this substance was mainly in the spotlight as a sleep aid and anaesthetic. Only later was it classified as a drug.

Although GHB occupies a small position in the Netherlands in terms of numbers of users, it is a drug that has attracted a remarkable amount of attention in recent years. As a "date rape drug", as an "ideal drug" and recently increasingly as a highly addictive and life-threatening drug. What is the truth about this? What is the truth around GHB? What is it, how does it work, and why has its reputation plummeted? Note: I don't have any knowledge on this substance nor do I have the answers on how this is in the rest of the world.

What does GHB do?

GHB, as mentioned above, stands for gammahydroxybutyric acid and occurs (even in non-users) in very small quantities in the human body. However, the concentration is so low that by international standards the substance cannot be considered "endogenous".

GHB is relatively easy to make yourself, with ingredents that can be easily ordered over the internet, such as GBL (largest ingredient in an industrial cleaner) and caustic soda (largest ingredient for sink plunger). Of course, this is then also not really healthy to put in your body.

GHB exists in powder form, but is most commonly found as a syrupy, colourless liquid. GHB has a narcotic effect on the central nervous system and gives a relaxed feeling; GHB is also sexually stimulating.

To recap:

GHB takes effect after about 5-30 minutes and the effect lasts for about 3 hours.

Use of GHB can produce the following effects:

- Relaxation
- Feeling happy
- Reduced anxiety
- Sensitivity to touch
- Sexual arousal

Where does GHB come from?

GHB was isolated in a laboratory in 1960 by French researcher Laborit. Surprisingly, it is still used as a drug for narcolepsy. Narcolepsy is a disease in which people are sleepy during the day and have sudden sleep attacks.

In the 1980s, the drug became popular among bodybuilders. From 1993 to 1996, GHB was sold in smartshops. From this period GHB also became popular in nightlife. In 2002, GHB was placed on list 2 of the Opium Act and in 2012 GHB was moved to list 1.

The Opium Act works with two lists of drugs. List I contains drugs with an unacceptable risk, also called hard drugs (such as cocaine, amphetamine, MDMA (XTC), heroin and LSD). List II includes drugs whose risks are lower than those of the drugs on list I, also called soft drugs. Examples include cannabis products, mushrooms and sleep aids (benzodiazepines).

The law then distinguishes between different acts that are punishable. Criminal acts are: possession, preparation or production, sale and export. Interestingly, use is not punishable.

Criminal acts must be detected and punished. The law specifies the penalty levels. Top prosecutors (the public prosecutors) also issue so-called guidelines. These guidelines describe which offences the police should give most thought to and what punishment can be given.

The Opium Act does allow use of drugs for medical and scientific purposes. So if an anaesthetist numbs a cancer patient's pain with morphine, this is not prohibited. However, a doctor or pharmacist must perform all kinds of administrative actions and there is strict control.

The Opium Act also lists substances for which we do not easily think of a drug, but rather medicines. (source: Jellinek)

These are medicines that can easily be misused as drugs, such as the sleeping drug Rohypnol (flunitrazepam). So this drug cannot be prescribed just like that. More about Rohypnol in the relevant chapter.

Please note that these numbers and laws pertain specifically to the Netherlands. I am not knowledgeable about laws in other countries.

Side effects of GHB

Any stimulant or drug can have unwanted effects. GHB can cause nausea, dizziness, muscle weakness and convulsions in the face, legs and arms. But what makes GHB really (life)dangerous is that it is very difficult to dose.

The difference between an effective dose and an overdose is extremely small. With an overdose, unconsciousness or even a coma can quickly occur, with respiration being suppressed (especially in combination with other substances such as alcohol).

GHB is also highly addictive. After only a few weeks of frequent use, the GHB user can become dependent. Because GHB only works for a short time, dependent users have to take a new dose every two to four hours - day and night - to avoid withdrawal symptoms. Often paired with speed or other type of Upper so they stay awake.

These withdrawal symptoms are another reason why GHB is so dangerous: suddenly stopping GHB can cause very serious and even life-threatening complications, with delirium, seizures, hypertension and hallucinations. Stopping GHB on your own, without supervision, is therefore strongly discouraged.

Rohypnol

Rohypnol® is the brand name of a strong sleep aid with the active ingredient flunitrazepam. As a sleep aid, the drug is almost no longer prescribed. Rohypnol (also called the red tuber) was also used as a drug by drug users.

What is Rohypnol?

Rohypnol falls under the group of benzodiazepines which includes most sleep and sedatives such as Mogadon, Dalmadorm, Valium, Temesta and Seresta. Benzodiazepines have muscle relaxant, anxiety-reducing and de-stressing effects.

What is Rohypnol used for?

Rohypnol was prescribed for severe sleep disorders that interfere with normal functioning or are suffered from. Currently, it is prescribed only in some exceptional cases. Because of its side effects, other sleep aids are always preferred.

What does Rohypnol do?

Benzodiazepines enhance the inhibitory effect of the neurotransmitter GABA. Neurotransmitters are substances in the brain that play a role in stimulus transmission. By enhancing the inhibitory effect of GABA, stimulus transmission in various parts of the brain is additionally inhibited. Rohypnol is absorbed quickly and starts working after only 10 to 20 minutes.

Side effects of Rohypnol

Rohypnol side effects include daytime sleepiness, muscle weakness, dizziness, confusion, fatigue and double vision. Memory loss may also occur, especially when combined with alcohol. In overdose, breathing is suppressed and one may go into a coma.

Addiction

Rohypnol is mentally and physically addictive. When quitting, you may experience withdrawal symptoms such as headaches, muscle aches, confusion, hallucinations and cramps.

Rohypnol as a drug

Rohypnol was popular for a time in the hard drug scene, where people used the 'rooie knol' (Dutch name translates as ginger turnip) not as a sleeping drug but as an intoxicant. People tried to stay awake after taking it and enter a kind of dream state. Users felt sedated but also noticed that afterwards they could not remember what had happened. Currently, drug addiction is a reason for doctors to stop prescribing rohypnol.

Other risks

Rohypnol in combination with alcohol or drugs can be life-threatening, leading to self-aggrandisement, aggression, disinhibition, total amnesia and overdose. Some psychiatrists believe that certain violent crimes were due to abuse of this drug.

You were never created to live depressed, guilty, condemned, ashamed or unworthy.

You were created to be victorious.

- Joel Osteen

Chapter 5: How does your brain work?

And why does it matter?

Before I get into the symptoms, I need to devote a chapter to the brain. How does it work? And what affects it all? Because how information is kt and the effect of trauma or stress in your brain has a huge effect on what you feel, what you do and what you think.

So now first a bit of theory about how your brain works.

Information processing in the brain

The part of your brain responsible for putting facts away is the Hippocampus. This part maps the collective facts and impressions and places them into a meaningful whole. It then stores the facts and impressions. If you take a computer as an example, memories are stored by, for example, place, birthdays or people. You could then say that because of the trauma, the computer does not recognise the facts such as place, subject, face, etc. and does not know which folder to put the information away in.

In the Almond nucleus, the Amygdala, the emotions and sensory impressions come in and determine which are important or not and attach emotions to them. Feeling information is also stored here. In other words; the Amygdala encodes the emotions and the Hippocampus the context.

Because memories and emotions from this trauma have not found a matching folder, they therefore cannot be put away properly either and remain "stuck" in the brain as unprocessed. As a result, the feelings and thoughts also remain so "present". And because these emotions are so present, they also keep sending signals to the nerve cells. As if the fact is happening again and again. This is also a reason why people with trauma often relive.

The nerve cells in the brain give off signals with substances (neurotransmitters) and bursts of steam (impulses) that can be compared to small electrical currents of about 0.07 volts. So the brain is constantly under electricity and it doesn't know where to send the signals. It cannot find a folder where it should go. At some point it becomes too many.

My assumption is that because of the many surges of power, the surrounding areas are also continuously affected because the energy cannot be released in the normal way. After all, energy does not go to waste. This negative cycle can eventually cause stress-related symptoms again.

So, these unprocessed emotions and thoughts, the dust and power surges, have a great impact on the surrounding areas in the brain because signals are continuously being issued in the brain. The information is too much, too many signals enter the brain, the neurotransmitters and electric current surges eventually cause a kind of short circuit. Therefore, the neurotransmitters, as mentioned, over time also affect the nearest areas of the brain and signal "Malfunction" there too. So what are those adjacent areas and what do they take care of? You can read more about that, in the following chapter.

Effects on the hippocampus

The effects of prolonged stress and overactivity on the brain has several consequences. For example, it can cause the Hippocampus to shrink. When you consider that the Hippocampus is responsible for stored facts, and if a shrunken Hippocampus can no longer function properly, it may just affect your memory. But it also regulates how you react to certain situations, which may cause you to behave differently than you were used to. For example, that you start crying very loudly when you suddenly enter a traffic jam.

Damage to and/or shrinkage of the Hippocampus may bring the following symptoms:

- Memory loss,
- Problems with imprinting and storage,
- Problems with memorisation and long-term memory,
- Disorientation,

Shrinkage (or Atrophy) of the Hippocampus is also associated with:

- Depression,
- Bipolar disorder,
- Schizophrenia.

It is said that "silence" can promote the production of new cells in the hippocampus.

People with lesions in this part of the brain often cannot name what they are anxious about when they are anxious, but can feel an unconscious reaction of fear.

Effects on the amygdala

The Amygdala is involved in the formation and storage of information related to emotional events. It processes the emotions associated with an event. It is also involved in storing in long-term memory. Also, the Amygdala helps distinguish when there is danger or something is frightening.

The effects of trauma on the Amygdala include:

- Disorders in memory formation
- Emotional sensitivity
- Problems in learning and remembering
- Depression and gloom
- Anxiety

An overactive Amygdala is also associated with a higher risk of cardiovascular disease. But also with PTSD (Post Traumatic Stress Disorder).

Effects on the pituitary gland

The pituitary gland is an organ or gland the size of a pea. It is an organ responsible for making various hormones and directs other glands that produce hormones. Hormones move through the blood. These hormones, including endorphins, regulate sensory stimuli, fine motor skills, consciousness and breathing, stress and emotions. If there is injury in this organ or it does not function properly, it directly affects functions elsewhere in the body.

During short-term stress, Adrenaline and Noradrenaline are produced. These hormones are very useful but again, excess damages.

Because Adrenaline and Noradrenaline cause fat breakdown, it seems logical to me that the layer of fat around the nerve cells is also affected. This layer of fat provides insulation, just like around an electrical wire and prevents short circuits. So with prolonged exposure to stress where Adrenaline is released, there is more chance of short-circuiting. (However, I have not been able to establish or verify this and therefore it remains an assumption).

The following symptoms can result from a pituitary gland that is no longer functioning properly:

- More emotional behavior,
- Irritable,
- Mood swings,
- Depressed feelings,
- Decreased sexual desire,
- Concentration disorders,
- More sensitive to external stimuli,
- Memory problems.

When the pituitary gland is controlled by the Hypothalamus after a stressful event, several hormones are secreted including Adrenaline. If the stressful situation persists, the Pituitary stimulates the adrenal glands to start producing the hormone Cortisol. Cortisol is an important stress hormone but if these levels are too high it can have health consequences. This hormone is toxic to the brain and produces powerless thoughts, among other things. Cortisol has the effect of shrinking the Hippocampus and can cause reduced immunity and fatigue.

Cortisol is also associated with high cholesterol, increased risk of cardiovascular disease, arteriosclerosis, makes you want to eat more carbohydrates or fast fats/sugars to supply your body with energy (because you are so tired), diabetes, heartburn, spastic colon and it slows down the healing process.

Prolonged or chronic stress has so much effect on the brain and it can cause flared problems such as concentration problems, muscle tension pain, acne, hair loss, headaches, etc.

Surrounding areas of the brain

The Amygdala and the Hippocampus are part of the limbic system. The limbic system is formed by a group of brain structures in the cerebellum involved in emotion, emotion regulation, emotional memory, pleasure and motivation. If the Amygdala and the Hippocampus are under the influence of stress hormones Adrenaline and Cortisol for a long period of time, it also affects the adjacent areas of the brain. If you look at the surrounding areas of the Hippocampus and Amygdala, you will see that the sleep and wake centre is right next to it (midbrain) and therefore under the influence of stress can be a cause of her sleeping badly.

But the control of the hormonal system is also right next to it (pituitary gland), causing, for example, too much or too little hormones to be released into the blood. (See: The effects on the pituitary gland).

Also, under the influence of stress, the Hypothalamus may show poorer function. Among other things, the Hypothalamus is responsible for regulating your blood pressure. The Hypothalamus also has the task of controlling the hormonal system (pituitary gland) but can also release hormones itself. It also regulates the autonomic nervous system including breathing, heart rate, blood pressure and body temperature. It also regulates food intake, as well as hunger and thirst, sleep and wake rhythms.

The possible symptoms associated with damage to the Hypothalamus are:

- Lack of motivation,
- Altered sleep-wake rhythm,
- Altered menstrual pattern,
- Hyperactivity,
- Feelings of euphoria,
- Lack or excessive feelings of hunger or thirst.

The Thalamus is called the gateway to the cerebral cortex and is responsible for transmitting many sensory stimuli (except smell), but it also has to filter stimuli which, if you are healthy, allows you to 'shut off' for a moment when you are reading to sounds, for example. The thalamus is also associated with wakefulness and sleep, consciousness and wakefulness, motor skills and event-related emotions.

Damage to or a malfunctioning thalamus can cause the following symptoms:

- Facial field loss,
- Decreased taste,
- Decreased sensation of pain,
- Decreased sensation in one side of the body,
- Unable to find words,
- Apathy,
- Unable to stop an action or disengage from a particular thought
- Personality change,
- Overexcitement,
- Unable to distinguish main issues from side issues,
- Memory loss.

Chapter 6: Understanding Date Rape

Defining Date Rape

Date rape, also known as acquaintance rape or drug-facilitated sexual assault, is a type of sexual assault that occurs when the victim is drugged or incapacitated without their consent. It often happens during social situations, such as dates or parties, where the perpetrator takes advantage of the victim's vulnerable state. Date rape is a serious violation of trust and can have lasting consequences on the survivor's physical, emotional, and psychological well-being.

Research into the consequences of date rape has shown that survivors often experience a range of physical and emotional symptoms, including anxiety, depression, post-traumatic stress disorder (PTSD), and substance abuse. These symptoms can be debilitating and may impact the survivor's ability to function in daily life. It is important for survivors to seek support and professional help to address these issues and begin the healing process.

Recovery and healing processes for date rape survivors can be complex and challenging, but with the right support and resources, survivors can heal and reclaim their lives. Therapy, support groups, and self-care practices can all be helpful in the healing process. It is important for survivors to prioritize their own well-being and to surround themselves with supportive and understanding individuals who can help them navigate their healing journey.

Breaking the silence around date rape is crucial in empowering survivors to seek help and support. By sharing their stories and experiences, survivors can connect with others who have been through similar situations and find strength in solidarity. It is important for survivors to know that they are not alone and that there are resources available to help them heal and recover from the trauma of date rape.

In defining date rape, it is important to recognize that it is never the survivor's fault. Perpetrators are responsible for their actions, and survivors deserve to be believed, supported, and treated with empathy and respect. By breaking the silence and speaking out about date rape, survivors can advocate for change and raise awareness about the prevalence and impact of this form of sexual violence. Healing and recovery are possible, and survivors deserve to reclaim their sense of safety, autonomy, and dignity.

Statistics on Date Rape Incidents

In this subchapter, we will delve into the alarming statistics surrounding date rape incidents. According to research, it is estimated that 1 in 5 women will experience some form of sexual assault in their lifetime, with a significant portion of these cases involving date rape. This highlights the prevalence of this issue and emphasizes the importance of addressing it within our society.

Furthermore, studies have shown that a large percentage of date rape incidents involve the use of drugs or alcohol to incapacitate the victim. This is a particularly insidious form of sexual assault, as the victim may not even be aware of what has happened to them until after the fact. It is crucial for women to be vigilant and cautious when it comes to accepting drinks or substances from others, especially in social settings where they may be more vulnerable.

The consequences of date rape can be devastating and long-lasting. Victims often experience feelings of shame, guilt, and self-blame, which can hinder their healing and recovery process. In addition, survivors may struggle with trust issues, intimacy issues, and post-traumatic stress disorder (PTSD) as a result of their traumatic experience. It is essential for survivors to seek support and therapy to address these issues and move towards healing.

Recovery and healing processes for date rape survivors are unique to each individual, but they often involve therapy, support groups, and self-care practices. It is important for survivors to prioritize their mental and emotional well-being and to seek help from trained professionals who can guide them through the healing process. By breaking the silence and speaking out about their experiences, survivors can begin to reclaim their power and take steps towards healing and recovery.

In conclusion, the statistics on date rape incidents are sobering, but they also shed light on the urgent need for awareness, prevention, and support for survivors. It is crucial for women who have been drugged and suffered a date rape to know that they are not alone and that help is available. By coming together as a community, we can work towards breaking the cycle of silence and stigma surrounding date rape, and support survivors on their journey towards healing and recovery.

Common Misconceptions About Date Rape

Date rape is a serious and devastating crime that can happen to anyone, regardless of their age, gender, or sexual orientation. Unfortunately, there are many misconceptions surrounding date rape that can prevent survivors from seeking help and healing. In this subchapter, we will address some of the common misconceptions about date rape and provide information to help survivors navigate their recovery process.

One common misconception about date rape is that it is only considered rape if the victim physically resists the attacker. This is simply not true. Consent must be freely given, and if someone is unable to give consent due to being drugged or incapacitated, then any sexual activity that occurs is considered rape. It is important for survivors to know that they are not at fault for what happened to them, regardless of whether they were able to physically resist their attacker.

Another misconception is that date rape only occurs between strangers in dark alleys. In reality, the majority of date rape cases involve perpetrators who are known to the victim, such as friends, acquaintances, or romantic partners. This can make it even more difficult for survivors to come forward, as they may fear retaliation or disbelief from those they know. It is important for survivors to know that they are not alone and that there are resources available to help them heal and recover.

Some people believe that if a survivor was drinking or using drugs at the time of the assault, then they are partially to blame for what happened to them. This victim-blaming mentality is harmful and can prevent survivors from seeking the help they need. It is important for survivors to know that no one ever deserves to be violated or assaulted, regardless of their state of intoxication. Recovery and healing are possible for all survivors, regardless of the circumstances surrounding their assault.

Many people believe that date rape is not a serious crime and that survivors should just "get over it" and move on with their lives. This mindset can be incredibly damaging to survivors, as it minimizes the trauma and pain they have experienced. It is important for survivors to know that their feelings are valid and that seeking help and support is a crucial step in their healing process. By breaking the silence and speaking out about their experiences, survivors can begin to reclaim their power and find healing and recovery.

Chapter 7: Research on the Consequences of a Date Rape

Psychological Effects of Date Rape

Date rape, also known as drug-facilitated sexual assault, can have profound psychological effects on survivors. Research into the consequences of date rape has shown that survivors often experience feelings of shame, guilt, and self-blame. These feelings can lead to depression, anxiety, and post-traumatic stress disorder (PTSD). Survivors may also struggle with trust issues, intimacy issues, and difficulties forming healthy relationships in the aftermath of a date rape.

Recovery and healing processes for date rape survivors can be complex and challenging. It is important for survivors to seek support from trained professionals, such as therapists and counselors, who can help them navigate the emotional aftermath of a date rape. Therapy can provide survivors with a safe space to process their feelings, explore coping strategies, and develop skills for managing trauma triggers. Support groups can also be beneficial for survivors, as they provide an opportunity to connect with others who have had similar experiences and validate their feelings.

One common psychological effect of date rape is a sense of powerlessness and loss of control. Survivors may struggle with feelings of helplessness, vulnerability, and fear of future victimization. These feelings can impact survivors' sense of self-worth and self-esteem, making it difficult for them to reclaim their agency and autonomy. It is important for survivors to work through these feelings in therapy and develop strategies for rebuilding their sense of empowerment and self-confidence.

Another psychological effect of date rape is a profound sense of betrayal and violation. Survivors may struggle with feelings of anger, resentment, and mistrust towards others, particularly those in positions of authority or trust. These feelings can impact survivors' ability to form healthy relationships and establish boundaries with others. Therapy can help survivors explore these feelings, process their trauma, and develop skills for rebuilding trust and intimacy in their relationships.

Ultimately, the psychological effects of date rape can be devastating, but with the right support and resources, survivors can heal and recover. It is important for survivors to prioritize self-care, seek professional help, and connect with others who can provide support and understanding. By acknowledging their experiences, processing their feelings, and developing healthy coping strategies, survivors can begin the journey towards healing and reclaiming their lives.

The complaints I saw in this client and which she described to me can be divided into various physical complaints and mental complaints. So this description is specifically about this client but various studies on trauma have shown similar outcomes.

The psychological symptoms and impact of the incident are great. She feels a lot of shame and suffers from anxiety. In addition, she has low self-esteem and no longer trusts men. Especially men in suits. In addition, she has periods with depressive feelings and crying fits, she feels very insecure and it is sometimes difficult to get out of it. She also suffers from nightmares. A doctor has given her a diagnosis of "Generalized Anxiety Disorder".

The client already has a history of depression and self-mutilation. This remains a risk of possible relapse and certainly very important to keep monitoring. She would prefer to forget and put the incident behind her. She feels jaded and lost. When told about this, she says she finds it difficult to ask for help. That she feels out of touch with herself.

In company, she feels unwanted and out of touch. However, she is highly motivated to work on herself. She wants to become more confident and learn to trust men again. She wants to gain more insight into her process and save others from what she went through.

The various complaints may be caused by the trauma but may also recognize effects attributable to drug administration. Also, there may be complaints that are not necessarily the result of the trauma but due to past events.

These complaints may worsen or become more visible due to the trauma. For example, old beliefs "I'm not worth anything, I don't matter, etc." may be triggered even more by this trauma.

Or "You see, my boundaries don't matter, people I trust can hurt you, etc."

Anxiety complaints

One complaint the client suffers from is Anxiety. If you look at how the brain works, we can also explain these complaints, as described as a complaint of a poorly functioning Amygdala. So does this fall under Psychological complaint or physical complaint?

Research has shown that the Hippocampus and Amygdala have a large share in causing various anxiety disorders. The reflex or innate emotion Anxiety is attributed to the Amygdala. The information to the amygdala goes through another structure located deep in your brain, the thalamus.

The thalamus relays information very quickly, but not completely. Its arrival in the amygdala triggers activation of anxiety.

So the information from the thalamus may be unjustified.

After some time, it is processed by a second fear system (hippocampus), which passes it back to the amygdala. This information is much more precise. More precise, but slower. Under the influence of overactivity, the emotion Fear may be triggered unjustly or too often. As a result, clients struggle with feelings of anxiety.

Another explanation for Anxiety might be based on the activities in the different brain hemispheres. A healthy brain has a certain balance in the functioning of both hemispheres. When your brain goes into survival mode, for example, your right hemisphere may take over. This side is responsible for emotions and feelings because the left part cannot process facts. But without balance, emotions and feelings can become overwhelming because the left half has no logical explanation. And the feelings and emotions are then sometimes disproportionate. Like the example of starting to cry very loudly when suddenly driving into a traffic jam.

There are various Anxiety Disorders and client has been diagnosed with Generalised Anxiety Disorder in which client suffers from prolonged excessive feelings of anxiety and worry that are difficult to control.

What is fear?

Fear is a normal reaction is to imminent danger. We can fear essential (external) danger, such as a natural disaster, or perceived (internal) danger, such as the fear of failure. Fear, like pain, has an important function; it is a signal that we must move to fight the danger (fight) or, on the contrary, escape it (flee). To this end, the heart speeds up (palpitations), breathing speeds up (hyperventilation) and extra blood goes to muscles used for running (getting warm).

What is Generalized Anxiety?

Everyone worries sometimes, and sometimes it is even useful. For example, worrying encourages you to prepare well for a situation in which you have to perform, such as an exam or a job interview.

People with generalized anxiety disorder have a vague and unreasonable fear of about all kinds of dangers that may take place in the future. They feel threatened, uneasy, agitated and have constant anxious anticipations of impending doom. They worry about all sorts of things, even though there is no reason for them. For instance, they worry about their studies, even though they are getting good results. About their health, even though nothing is wrong.

For them, brooding has become an automatic response to everyday problems. They are worried, anxious, nervous and tense, find it difficult to control their anxiety and fretting, and worry about all kinds of small, day-to-day events. The anxiety and worry is accompanied by at least three of the following symptoms: restlessness, fatigue, difficulty concentrating, irritability, increased muscle tension, sleep problems.

Symptoms of Generalized Anxiety Disorder:

The DSM-IV (The DSM is a reference work that lists all diagnoses, what it should meet, what it can cause and where it can come from) classifies people with generalised anxiety disorder as people who are constantly worried about everyday things, which in turn trigger anxiety. The person in question knows the anxiety is exaggerated, but still cannot control it.

DSM-5 indicates excessive fear and anxiety (fearful premonitions) that are present more often than not for at least 6 months, and relate to a number of events or activities. The person finds it difficult to control the anxiety.

The fear and anxiety are accompanied by three (or more) of the following six symptoms:

- Restlessness; distended or tense feeling,
- Quickly fatigued,
- Difficulty concentrating,
- Irritability,
- Muscle tension,
- Sleep disorder.

So if in addition to the anxiety you experience 3 of the above physical symptoms are present for longer than 6 months we may speak of generalised anxiety disorder.

DSM-5 Generalized Anxiety Disorder 300.02

Below is the complete description from the DSM-5:

A. Excessive fear and anxiety (fearful premonitions), which are more frequent than not for at least six months, and relate to a number of events or activities.

B. Person finds it difficult to control anxiety.

C. The fear and anxiety are accompanied by three (or more) of the following six symptoms:

1. Restlessness; distended or tense feeling.
2. Getting tired quickly.
3. Irritability.
4. Muscle tension.
5. Sleep disorder.

D. Fear. anxiety or physical symptoms cause clinically significant suffering or impairment in social or occupational functioning or in functioning in other important areas.

E. The disorder cannot be better explained by another mental disorder.

Causes:

- Biological susceptibility, hereditary factors (30-40%)
- Personality and character
- Upbringing/experiences in childhood

e.g. overprotective and controlling upbringing, traumatic events such as abuse prolonged stress, drastic events

e.g. stress at work, physical illnesses, conflicts neurobiological dysfunctions of brain areas in the so-called brain-anxiety circuit. This is a network of brain regions involved in fear and fear responses (prefrontal cortex, amygdala, hippocampus). In this brain anxiety circuit, the neurotransmitters noradrenaline, serotonin, gamma-aminobutyric acid and glutamate are active. (source: hulpgids.nl)

Depressive complaints

My client also suffered from episodes of depressive complaints. Depressive complaints also have their origin in the memories and can be (partly) explained on the basis of the above. There are several causes for depression that I will not go into further because this is clearly a case of blocking painful feelings and thoughts due to an unprocessed traumatic experience leading to depression.

Symptoms of depression

Psychological Symptoms:

- Depressed mood: dejection, sadness, gloom, hopelessness, depression; sometimes this lowered mood is worst in the morning ("daytime swings")
- Fatigue, loss of energy, initiative and strength.
- Feeling: anxiety is often a characteristic feeling in depression; sometimes there is a strong flattening of emotional life: one no longer feels anything, no sadness, joy, fear or joy.
- Disorders of the form of thinking: problems with concentration and memory, thinking inhibition and indecisiveness.
- Thoughts of guilt, self-blame, worthlessness and loss of self-respect.

Behavioral symptoms:

- Social withdrawal behaviour, loss of interest in surroundings
- Loss of ability to experience pleasure
- Physical restlessness or just inhibited behaviour
- Reduced productivity
- Suicidality (suicidal thoughts/needs)
- Bouts of crying

Functional symptoms (vital or biological functions):

- Eating disorders: decreased or increased appetite
- Sleep disorders: sleep-in/out disorders, early waking, or sleepiness
- Sexual disorders: reduced desire (libido over-lie)
- Physical complaints: constipation or diarrhea

Psychotic Symptoms:

Psychotic features are present in 10-15% of depression, i.e. there is a disturbed scrutiny of reality. In psychotic depression, this usually manifests as delusions (uncorrectable thought processes). Often the content of these delusions is consistent with the depressive mood (mood congruent): the themes centre on personal shortcomings, failure, guilt, death, punishment or nihilism.

Low self-esteem

Client already suffered from low self-esteem in the past and this incident has reinforced that feeling. She feels she is worth nothing. She suffers tremendously from feelings of guilt. She does not feel strong and is out of sorts.

The incident exacerbated and rekindled this feeling. It gave her proof that she is worth nothing and that she can be so used and left like trash in a hotel room....

Physical Consequences of Date Rape

One of the most common physical consequences of date rape is the presence of injuries such as bruises, cuts, and abrasions. These injuries can be a result of physical force used during the assault or the survivor's attempts to resist the attack. Survivors may also experience soreness and pain in their genital area, as well as other parts of their body, due to the violent nature of the assault.

In addition to physical injuries, survivors of date rape may also experience long-term health consequences. Research has shown that survivors of sexual assault are at an increased risk for a variety of health issues, including chronic pain, gynecological problems, and sexually transmitted infections. Survivors may also experience psychological symptoms such as anxiety, depression, and post-traumatic stress disorder, which can have a significant impact on their overall well-being.

Recovery and healing from the physical consequences of date rape can be a long and challenging process. Survivors may require medical treatment for their injuries, as well as ongoing therapy to address the emotional and psychological impact of the assault. It is important for survivors to seek support from trained professionals, such as counselors and therapists, who can help them navigate the healing process and work through their trauma.

One important aspect of recovery for survivors of date rape is self-care and self-compassion. Survivors should prioritize their physical and emotional well-being by engaging in activities that promote healing, such as exercise, meditation, and journaling. It is also important for survivors to surround themselves with supportive and understanding individuals who can provide comfort and validation during this difficult time.

Ultimately, the physical consequences of date rape can have a profound impact on survivors, both physically and emotionally. It is crucial for survivors to seek help and support as they navigate the healing process and work towards reclaiming their sense of self-worth and empowerment. By breaking the silence surrounding date rape and speaking out about their experiences, survivors can begin to heal and move forward towards a brighter future.

When I ask the client about physical complaints, the thing that bothers her most is that she is constantly feeling exhausted. She also mentions that she struggles to get a good night's sleep, often experiencing a heaviness in her head, eyes, and chest.

The impact of trauma is evident through the various stress-related symptoms she is experiencing. It is clear that the process of properly addressing and processing the trauma, both the facts and the emotions associated with it, has not yet been completed by her brain.

The stress stemming from the trauma, the overwhelming sadness, the desire to forget what happened while being unable to do so, the confusion about the events, the lingering uncertainty, and other unprocessed emotions are all causing distress that the brain is struggling to handle in its usual manner.

The normal way means that memories and emotions are basically put away in a place in the brain where it is appropriate. As explained earlier how you do that on the computer, for example: you store items in various folders by category such as photos, movies or documents. Or categorised by event such as holiday, work or birthday. So something similar happens in your brain too.

For instance, you have a place in your head for parties, birthdays, holidays, family, pets, friends, etc. In this way, your brain also creates a kind of files. So your head has several drawers, with various contents.

A trauma basically has no place. So that's what makes putting it away so difficult.

Page 58

It's often just enough to be with someone.

I don't need to touch them.

Not even talk.

A feeling passes between you both.

You're not alone.

- Marilyn Monroe

Social and Emotional Impact of Date Rape

Date rape is a traumatic experience that can have lasting social and emotional impacts on survivors. Research into the consequences of date rape has shown that survivors often experience feelings of shame, guilt, and self-blame. These feelings can lead to isolation and a reluctance to seek help or support from others. Survivors may also struggle with feelings of anger, fear, and betrayal, as well as difficulty trusting others. The emotional impact of date rape can be overwhelming, and it is important for survivors to understand that they are not alone in their experiences.

Recovery and healing processes for date rape survivors are complex and can vary from person to person. It is important for survivors to seek support from trained professionals who can help them navigate their emotions and begin the healing process.

Therapy, support groups, and other forms of counseling can be valuable tools for survivors as they work through their trauma and begin to rebuild their lives. It is also important for survivors to take care of themselves physically, emotionally, and mentally as they heal from the trauma of date rape.

One of the key challenges that date rape survivors face is overcoming the stigma and shame associated with their experiences. Many survivors may feel that they are to blame for what happened to them, or that they should have been able to prevent the assault. These feelings can be incredibly damaging and can prevent survivors from seeking the help and support they need to heal. It is important for survivors to remember that they are not at fault for what happened to them, and that they deserve compassion, understanding, and support as they work through their trauma.

The social impact of date rape can be significant, as survivors may struggle with feelings of shame, embarrassment, and fear of judgment from others. Survivors may also face challenges in their relationships with friends, family members, and romantic partners as they work through their trauma. It is important for survivors to communicate their needs and boundaries to others, and to seek out relationships that are supportive, understanding, and respectful. Building a strong support network of trusted individuals can be instrumental in helping survivors navigate the emotional challenges of date rape and begin the healing process.

In conclusion, the social and emotional impact of date rape can be profound and long-lasting. Survivors may experience a range of emotions, including shame, guilt, anger, fear, and betrayal, as they work through their trauma.

Recovery and healing processes for date rape survivors are complex and can vary from person to person, but seeking support from trained professionals and building a strong support network can be invaluable tools for survivors as they navigate their healing journey. It is important for survivors to remember that they are not alone in their experiences, and that they deserve compassion, understanding, and support as they work through the aftermath of date rape.

Chapter 8: The Recovery Process

Seeking Support and Counseling

Seeking support and counseling is a crucial step in the healing and recovery process for women who have been drugged and suffered a date rape. It is important to remember that you are not alone in this experience and that there are resources available to help you navigate the complex emotions and trauma that may arise from such a violation. Research into the consequences of date rape has shown that survivors often experience a range of physical, emotional, and psychological symptoms, including anxiety, depression, PTSD, and substance abuse. Seeking support from trained professionals can help you address these issues and begin the healing process.

Counseling can provide a safe space for you to process your feelings, explore coping strategies, and develop a sense of empowerment and control over your life. Therapists who specialize in working with survivors of sexual assault can offer evidence-based interventions to help you manage symptoms and work towards healing. Support groups can also be a valuable resource, providing a sense of community and understanding from others who have had similar experiences.

Recovery and healing processes for date rape survivors are unique to each individual, and it is important to find what works best for you. Some survivors may find solace in creative outlets such as art therapy or journaling, while others may benefit from mindfulness practices like yoga or meditation. It is important to listen to your own needs and desires as you navigate this challenging journey towards healing.

In addition to individual therapy and support groups, reaching out to loved ones for support can also be incredibly beneficial. Building a strong support network of friends and family members who believe and validate your experiences can help you feel less isolated and more understood. It is important to remember that you deserve to be treated with respect and compassion, and that seeking help is a courageous step towards reclaiming your sense of self-worth and agency.

Remember, healing from date rape is a process that takes time and patience. It is okay to take things one day at a time and to seek support whenever you need it. You are a survivor, and you deserve to live a life free from the burden of trauma. By seeking support and counseling, you are taking an important step towards reclaiming your power and finding healing and recovery.

Self-Care Strategies for Healing

As a survivor of date rape, it is crucial to prioritize your own self-care in order to begin the healing process. Research into the consequences of date rape has shown that survivors often experience feelings of shame, guilt, and self-blame. It is important to remember that these feelings are a natural response to trauma and that you are not alone in experiencing them. By implementing self-care strategies, you can begin to slowly work through these emotions and move towards a place of healing and recovery.

One of the most important self-care strategies for date rape survivors is to seek out professional help. Therapy can be a powerful tool in processing the trauma of date rape and working through the complex emotions that come with it. A trained therapist can help you develop coping mechanisms and provide a safe space for you to explore your feelings without judgment. Additionally, support groups for survivors of sexual assault can provide a sense of community and understanding that can be incredibly healing.

In addition to seeking professional help, it is important to take care of your physical health in the aftermath of date rape. Make sure to prioritize regular exercise, healthy eating, and plenty of rest. Engaging in activities that bring you joy and relaxation, such as yoga or meditation, can also be beneficial in reducing stress and anxiety. Remember to listen to your body and give yourself the time and space you need to heal.

Another important self-care strategy for date rape survivors is to practice self-compassion. It is common for survivors to blame themselves for the assault or to feel unworthy of love and support. By cultivating self-compassion, you can begin to challenge these negative beliefs and treat yourself with kindness and understanding. Remember that you are not to blame for what happened to you and that you deserve to be treated with respect and dignity.

Finally, it is important to set boundaries in your relationships and prioritize your own needs. Date rape survivors often struggle with feelings of powerlessness and a loss of control, so it is important to assert your boundaries and communicate your needs to others. Surround yourself with supportive and understanding people who respect your boundaries and provide you with the love and care you deserve. By prioritizing your own self-care, you can begin to heal from the trauma of date rape and move towards a place of strength, empowerment, and ultimately, a renewed sense of self-worth.

Building a Support Network

Building a Support Network is a crucial step in the healing and recovery process for women who have been drugged and suffered a date rape. Research into the consequences of date rape has shown that survivors often experience feelings of shame, guilt, and isolation. It is important for survivors to realize that they are not alone in their struggle and that there are people who care about them and want to help.

One of the first things survivors should do is reach out to trusted friends and family members for support. These individuals can provide emotional support, as well as practical help with things like finding a therapist or attending support group meetings. It is important for survivors to surround themselves with people who will listen without judgment and offer unconditional love and support.

In addition to friends and family, survivors can also benefit from connecting with other survivors of date rape through support groups or online forums. These spaces provide a safe and understanding environment where survivors can share their experiences, receive validation, and gain insight into their own healing journey. Building connections with others who have gone through similar experiences can be incredibly empowering and validating.

Therapy is another important component of building a support network for date rape survivors. A therapist can provide survivors with the tools and resources they need to process their trauma, cope with their emotions, and develop healthy coping mechanisms. Therapy can also help survivors work through feelings of shame and self-blame, and learn to trust in themselves and others again.

Ultimately, building a support network is about creating a safe and nurturing environment where survivors can heal and grow. By reaching out to trusted individuals, connecting with other survivors, and seeking professional help, survivors can begin to rebuild their lives and move forward on their journey of healing and recovery. Remember, you are not alone, and there are people who care about you and want to help you through this difficult time.

Chapter 9: Treatment and possible interventions

What actions are advisable and which ones should be avoided?

The most important thing in recovery after a trauma like this, a possible sexual assault or rape after administering a drug, is to give clients back their sense of "power".

"The core experiences of psychological trauma are powerlessness and isolation. The survivor's recovery, therefore, relies on data that she regains power and feels reconnected to others. Recovery is only possible within the context of relationships; it cannot take place in isolation." This is as it is described in Judith Herman's book Trauma & Recovery. This principle of giving back control to the traumatised person is fairly widely recognised. Several therapists subscribe to this theory such as Abram Kardiner and Martin Symonds.

Evan Stark 15 and Anne Flitcraft cite the restoration of autonomy and power the goal of their therapeutic work with abused women.

The primary focus of this treatment is therefore restoring self-esteem and regaining one's own power. It is also important to look at carrying capacity. In the first sessions, the client's carrying capacity was not that great. A possible relapse into depression was very likely.

Herman also writes about the well-meaning attempts that are made to help the victim but which do not take this power restoration into account, and this is why it does not work.

In the words of an incest survivor: 'Good therapists were the ones who really gave credence to my experiences and helped me get a grip on my behavior instead of trying to get a grip on me. ' Some social workers accustomed to a medical treatment model, a vasified treatment protocol and often struggle to understand and put into practice this fundamental principle (restoration of power).

From the working method of integrative therapist as I practise the profession, this is actually quite appropriate and logical for me. By asking "What is bothering you right now?" you can very well deploy an intervention on what is going on right now. As a matter of course, you end up where it comes from. No matter how big or small the trauma or memory. In principle, it doesn't matter.

Another premise I use is, that for strengthening the desired state, you can activate these nerve pathways and make them stronger with the help of imagination. Indeed, for the brain, it is irrelevant whether this situation is real or an imagination. The white matter surrounding the nerve cells becomes visibly thicker and thus stronger. The thicker, the sooner this (new) pathway will be used.

In sports, this technique has been used for years. Athletes do their race, play their match before it is played with a visualisation of how it could be. How they grab that extra time, how they jump an inch higher or how they get the that bit faster. In this way, the white matter surrounding the nerve cells visibly thickens and strengthens like a muscle. This has been demonstrated by science. So their brain will know exactly what to do when it actually happens because it has already run the race.

This is another reason why hypnotherapy can work so well because it also works with imagination and the client's imagination.

Therefore, hypnotherapy is helpful in many ways. You can use imagination to let the client "solve" a lot himself and meanwhile give positive suggestions to the unconscious for, for instance, healing, growth, peace and strength.

The cell structures visibly change and the client will be able to feel better and better. Not only because of the beautiful healing but certainly also by improving the functioning of the nerve cells.

Possible interventions listed

Below is an overview of the possible interventions that can help treat trauma without memory.

1. Self-image strengthening through various solution-focused exercises and NLP.

2. Social Panorama (Lucas Derks)

3. Hypnosis. Regaining power, " moving " emotions and memories to the right place in the brain.

4. Regression. Returning power. Karmic exchange.

5. Cognitive Behavioral Therapy.

6. ACT (Acceptance and Commitment Therapy).

7. Mindfulness/Meditation/Yoga

1. As mentioned, I started working on strengthening self-esteem first. I did several exercises to give her insight into where she is now and where she would like to go. Current State and Desired State questioning, Scales exercise (where are you now and where do you want to go?), go do fun things (for the production of the happiness hormone), go for a walk (formation of neurons in the brain and improving the connections between brain cells) homework: writing, regaining a sense of strength and using symbols to anchor. Also give all space for and to her feelings.

Entirely spontaneously and as if by itself, memories suddenly came back to her. Incidentally, not during a session. Two brief moments she could suddenly remember. And then the memory was more the feeling than actually an image. I did not make her recall any memories during the sessions (yet). However, I did compliment her for apparently feeling space to admit something.

I also saw that she was having a really hard time with this and indicated to her that we don't have to deal with this right away. That she has control over this process. This too was a conscious choice for me. As a victim, I want to give her back precisely that power and control. After all, that is also the objective. She chose to leave it because she didn't feel strong enough at that moment.

2. Another exercise I plan to do with her is Social Panorama. (Lucas Derks) And then in particular with the place of the offender in her panorama. But expressing any anger can also be done very nicely with this form of intervention. Returning power, and reinforcing that through imagining to a new situation to influence the nervous system and increase the white matter in the brain to the desired state. That too will have a positive impact on the whole.

3. As mentioned earlier, hypnosis is ideally suited to work with the unconscious. I am thinking here particularly of processing emotions, giving them a place. Releasing negative emotions and ballast. But also (re)finding strength, resources in the form of symbols. What also fits beautifully within a hypno-session is swimming in healing water and cleansing the body under a waterfall. Especially if someone feels " filthy", this can be very healing for re-accepting the body and making it their own again.

4. Regression I also see as a possibility, because of the karmic exchange that can take place. As in hypnosis, here she can give back to the perpetrator all kinds of things that have come to her and that do not belong to her. And also take back what is hers, that which she has lost, been taken away or lost at that moment. Like for example Strength, Self-confidence, Autonomy, Carefreeness, etc

Regression is possible only when there is enough carrying capacity and she is ready for this. This is not helpful to begin with. From the book Handbook of Hypnotherapy: "When you start engaging in regression therapy, it is important to know more about the subject of remembering.

Generally, as a regression therapist, you work with releasing energy from memories. By reliving them, the client may discover that he no longer has to be afraid now.

He can also discover what limiting life lessons he learnt from the, often traumatic, event." Olgers also explains the difference between remembering and reliving. And about how science is now changing and research is being done on memories people have while their brains did not (brain death). He then cites studies by Pearsall and Claire on "new" memories after a donor transplant. It might make you reconsider your ideas about memories, how they are stored and how they are processed.

5. Cognitive Behavioural Therapy for increasing self-confidence and positivity. I use Cognitive Behavioural Therapy to focus on what went well. With this, I aim to reduce negative thoughts and depressive feelings.

What you focus on grows, so if you want positive thoughts to grow and there to be more positive feelings, you have to focus on these things. This is why I also give her homework in the form of finding things that make her happy. Also showing the small steps of progress, which give more self-confidence and therefore a better mood.

Please note that I believe it is important to combine CBT with some form of healing therapy. In my view, CBT alone may only provide temporary relief and the client may revert to old behaviors if the underlying core pain is not addressed.

6. ACT (Acceptance and Commitment Therapy) Learning to accept human suffering as an inevitable part of life. Applying to be more in the here and now.

Because if you are depressed, you are living in the past. If you are scared then you are living in the future. And if you have found your peace, then you are living in the now. Lao Tzu.

ACT gives my client tools and insight into the sense and nonsense of control. What if what you think is not what you are? What if your thoughts are just allowed to be thoughts again? That you don't have to push them away, don't have to change them or replace them with something else? ACT is a wonderful method for that. You are not your thoughts, you have them!

I won't go into detail about ACT, but when you are a therapist and if you're familiar with it, it will make perfect sense. If you're a victim, you can research it and if you think it could help, I'm sure you can find a therapist who offers this method.

7. Mindfulness/Meditation/Yoga/Music/Writing as a resource. She has done a lot in this area. Actually, I want her to rediscover these possibilities. Therefore, I let her experiment with these and find out what is comfortable for her. As homework, I have asked her to make more use of music and writing as an outlet.

She has done the Music course and may be able to make much more use of this. All these exercises are meant to give her back her self-esteem. To let her find her way back to who she was and what she liked. Most important is to connect with your client with this.

If your client does not like writing, there is little point in giving this as an assignment. Then it becomes a "must" and the aim is to use tools that are appropriate. So that the process becomes more pleasant and doesn't feel like school where you had to do all sorts of things you didn't really want to do and that every session feels like an exam.

There are surely many more interventions that are appropriate. The above is a personal choice tailored to this client and applied in the first few sessions I had with her. It is not meant to be a protocol. It may help you find an appropriate intervention or look at your own tools through a different lens.

If you can dream it, you can do it!

-Walt Disney

Chapter 10: Healing from Trauma

Understanding Trauma Responses

When a woman experiences date rape, her body and mind undergo a traumatic experience that can have lasting effects on her mental and emotional well-being. Understanding trauma responses is crucial in the recovery and healing process for survivors of date rape. Research into the consequences of date rape has shown that individuals may exhibit a range of trauma responses, including but not limited to feelings of shock, numbness, confusion, and disbelief.

One common trauma response experienced by survivors of date rape is dissociation, where the individual may feel disconnected from their body or emotions in order to cope with the overwhelming experience.

This can manifest as a sense of being outside of oneself or feeling as though the assault is happening to someone else. It is important for survivors to recognize and validate their feelings of dissociation as a normal response to trauma.

Another common trauma response is hypervigilance, where survivors may experience heightened anxiety, fear, and vigilance in order to protect themselves from potential harm. This can manifest as difficulty sleeping, irritability, and a constant feeling of being on edge. It is important for survivors to practice self-care and seek support from loved ones or mental health professionals to help manage these feelings.

Survivors of date rape may also experience feelings of shame, guilt, and self-blame as a result of the assault. It is important for survivors to understand that these feelings are not their fault and that they are not alone in their experience. Seeking therapy and support groups can help survivors process their feelings and work towards self-forgiveness and healing.

In order to heal and recover from the trauma of date rape, it is important for survivors to educate themselves on trauma responses and seek out resources and support that can help them navigate their healing journey. By understanding trauma responses and practicing self-compassion, survivors can begin to rebuild their sense of safety, trust, and empowerment in the aftermath of a traumatic experience. Remember, you are not alone, and there is hope for healing and recovery.

Coping Mechanisms for Trauma

Coping mechanisms for trauma are essential tools for date rape survivors as they navigate the difficult journey of healing and recovery. Research into the consequences of date rape has shown that survivors often experience a range of emotions, including fear, shame, guilt, and anger. These emotions can be overwhelming and make it challenging to move forward. However, by implementing coping mechanisms, survivors can begin to process their trauma and work towards healing.

One effective coping mechanism for trauma is seeking professional help. Therapy can provide survivors with a safe space to explore their feelings and experiences, and can help them develop healthy coping strategies. A therapist can also provide valuable resources and support, and can assist survivors in addressing any mental health issues that may arise as a result of the trauma.

Another coping mechanism for trauma is engaging in self-care practices. Taking care of oneself is crucial for survivors as they work through their trauma. This may include practicing mindfulness, engaging in physical activity, getting enough rest, and eating well. Self-care can help survivors feel more grounded and connected to themselves, and can provide a sense of empowerment during a time when they may feel helpless.

Connecting with other survivors can also be a valuable coping mechanism for trauma. Support groups and online communities can provide survivors with a sense of belonging and understanding, and can help them feel less alone in their experiences. By sharing their stories and listening to others, survivors can gain strength and inspiration as they work towards healing.

Furthermore, engaging in creative outlets can be a powerful coping mechanism for trauma. Writing, art, music, and other forms of self-expression can help survivors process their emotions and experiences in a healthy way.

Creative outlets can also provide a sense of catharsis and empowerment, and can help survivors reclaim their voices and identities in the wake of trauma. By implementing these coping mechanisms, date rape survivors can begin to heal and recover from their experiences, and can find hope and healing in the midst of darkness. It is important to remember that healing is a journey, and by utilizing these coping mechanisms, survivors can take steps towards a brighter future filled with self-love and resilience.Moving Towards Recovery

Research into the consequences of date rape has shown that survivors often experience a range of physical, emotional, and psychological effects in the aftermath of the assault. These can include feelings of shame, guilt, fear, and self-blame, as well as symptoms of post-traumatic stress disorder (PTSD) such as flashbacks, nightmares, and anxiety.

Moving towards recovery after experiencing a traumatic event like date rape can be a long and challenging journey. However, it is important to remember that healing is possible, and there are resources and support available to help you through this difficult time.

Recovery and healing processes for date rape survivors often involve a combination of therapy, support groups, and self-care practices.

Therapy can help survivors process their trauma, identify and challenge negative thought patterns, and learn coping strategies for dealing with triggers and distressing emotions. Support groups provide a safe space for survivors to connect with others who have had similar experiences, share their stories, and receive validation and support from their peers. Self-care practices such as mindfulness, exercise, journaling, and relaxation techniques can also be helpful in managing symptoms and promoting healing.

It is important for survivors to prioritize their own well-being and take the time they need to heal at their own pace. This may involve setting boundaries with others, practicing self-compassion, and seeking out activities and relationships that bring joy and fulfillment. It is also important to remember that healing is not a linear process and that there may be setbacks along the way. It is normal to have good days and bad days, and it is okay to seek help and support when needed.

As you move towards recovery, it is important to remember that you are not alone. There are many organizations, hotlines, and support services available to help you through this difficult time. It is also important to surround yourself with people who believe and support you, and who can offer empathy, validation, and encouragement. Remember that healing is possible, and that with time, patience, and support, you can reclaim your sense of self-worth, rebuild your trust in others, and find peace and healing after experiencing date rape.

Chapter 11: Reclaiming Power and Agency

Empowerment through Self-Defense

In the aftermath of experiencing a traumatic event like date rape, it is not uncommon for survivors to feel overwhelmed, vulnerable, and powerless. However, it is crucial for women who have been drugged and suffered a date rape to reclaim their sense of empowerment through self-defense. Research into the consequences of date rape has shown that feeling empowered and in control of one's body can significantly aid in the healing and recovery process.

Self-defense training can provide date rape survivors with the tools and skills necessary to protect themselves in potentially dangerous situations.

By learning techniques to defend against physical attacks and practicing assertiveness in setting boundaries, survivors can regain a sense of agency over their own bodies. This newfound confidence can help survivors navigate the world with a greater sense of safety and security.

In addition to physical self-defense skills, empowerment through self-defense also involves developing mental and emotional resilience. Survivors are often burdened with feelings of shame, guilt, and self-blame following a date rape. By practicing self-compassion, challenging negative beliefs, and learning to trust their instincts, survivors can begin to rebuild their self-esteem and self-worth.

Furthermore, self-defense training can serve as a form of empowerment that extends beyond the individual survivor.

By sharing their knowledge and skills with other women in their communities, survivors can help prevent future incidents of date rape and contribute to creating a safer and more supportive environment for all. This sense of empowerment through community engagement can be a powerful tool in the healing and recovery process.

Ultimately, empowerment through self-defense is not just about physical protection, but about reclaiming one's sense of agency, autonomy, and dignity. By taking proactive steps to prioritize their safety and well-being, date rape survivors can begin to break free from the silence and shame that often accompanies their trauma. Through self-defense, survivors can transform their experiences of victimization into opportunities for growth, healing, and empowerment.

Advocacy for Change

Advocacy for Change is an essential aspect of healing and recovery for women who have been drugged and suffered a date rape. It involves speaking out about the issue, raising awareness, and pushing for policy changes to prevent future incidents. By advocating for change, survivors can reclaim their power and work towards creating a safer world for themselves and others.

Research into the consequences of date rape is crucial for understanding the long-term effects of this traumatic experience. Studies have shown that survivors of date rape are more likely to suffer from mental health issues such as depression, anxiety, and post-traumatic stress disorder. By advocating for more research in this area, survivors can help shed light on the impact of date rape and inform treatment and support services.

Recovery and healing processes for date rape survivors can be a long and challenging journey. Advocacy for Change can play a key role in this process by providing a platform for survivors to share their stories, connect with others who have had similar experiences, and demand better support services. By advocating for changes in the way society views and responds to date rape, survivors can feel empowered and supported in their recovery.

One important aspect of advocacy for change is pushing for better education and prevention programs. By raising awareness about the warning signs of date rape, how to seek help, and how to support survivors, we can work towards creating a culture of consent and respect. Survivors can use their voices to advocate for these programs in schools, workplaces, and communities, ensuring that future generations are better equipped to prevent and respond to date rape.

In conclusion, advocacy for change is a powerful tool for healing and recovery for women who have been drugged and suffered a date rape. By speaking out, raising awareness, and pushing for policy changes, survivors can reclaim their power and work towards creating a safer world for themselves and others. Through research, education, and prevention efforts, survivors can advocate for a better future for themselves and future generations.

Reclaiming Sexuality and Intimacy

Reclaiming sexuality and intimacy after experiencing date rape can be an incredibly difficult and daunting task for survivors. The trauma and betrayal of having their boundaries violated in such a personal and intimate way can leave lasting scars on a person's psyche. However, it is possible to reclaim a sense of ownership over one's own body and sexuality through healing and recovery processes.

Research into the consequences of date rape has shown that survivors often experience a range of physical, emotional, and psychological effects in the aftermath of the assault. These can include feelings of shame, guilt, anxiety, depression, and PTSD. Many survivors also struggle with issues related to intimacy and sexuality, such as trust issues, fear of intimacy, and difficulty establishing healthy boundaries in relationships.

In order to reclaim their sense of sexuality and intimacy, survivors must first prioritize their own healing and recovery. This can involve seeking therapy, support groups, and other forms of professional help to address the trauma and work through the emotional pain of the assault. It is important for survivors to give themselves permission to grieve, to feel anger, and to process their emotions in a healthy way.

Recovery and healing processes for date rape survivors often involve reevaluating their beliefs and attitudes towards sexuality and intimacy. Survivors may need to challenge societal norms and expectations around sex and relationships, and redefine what healthy intimacy looks like for them. This can involve exploring their own desires, boundaries, and needs, and learning to communicate them effectively with partners.

Ultimately, reclaiming sexuality and intimacy is a deeply personal journey that each survivor must navigate in their own way and at their own pace. It is important for survivors to be patient and compassionate with themselves as they work through the layers of trauma and begin to rebuild a sense of trust and safety within themselves and with others. By prioritizing their own healing and recovery, survivors can begin to reclaim their sense of empowerment and agency over their own bodies and sexuality.

He who sees the small has insight.

He who abides in gentleness has strength.

- Lao-Tse

Chapter 12: Moving Forward

Setting Boundaries and Asserting Consent

Setting boundaries and asserting consent are crucial aspects of preventing and healing from date rape. Many survivors of date rape were drugged or incapacitated in some way, making it difficult for them to clearly communicate their boundaries and assert their consent. It is important for women to understand that they have the right to set boundaries and say no to any unwanted advances, regardless of the circumstances. By learning how to assert their boundaries and communicate their consent clearly, women can protect themselves from potential harm and regain a sense of control over their own bodies.

Research into the consequences of date rape has shown that survivors often experience a wide range of physical, emotional, and psychological effects. These can include feelings of shame, guilt, and self-blame, as well as symptoms of anxiety, depression, and post-traumatic stress disorder.

By setting boundaries and asserting consent, survivors can begin to regain a sense of agency and empowerment in their lives. This can help them to address and overcome the negative effects of their traumatic experiences, and move towards healing and recovery.

Recovery and healing processes for date rape survivors can be complex and challenging, but setting boundaries and asserting consent can be an important first step towards regaining a sense of safety and self-worth.

Survivors may benefit from seeking therapy or counseling to process their experiences, develop coping strategies, and learn how to set healthy boundaries in their relationships. It is also important for survivors to surround themselves with supportive friends and family members who can provide love and understanding as they navigate the healing process.

In addition to seeking professional help, survivors can also benefit from engaging in self-care practices that promote healing and self-compassion. This can include activities such as meditation, journaling, exercise, and spending time in nature. By taking care of their physical, emotional, and spiritual well-being, survivors can begin to rebuild their sense of self and reclaim their agency and autonomy. Setting boundaries and asserting consent is an important part of this process, as it allows survivors to establish healthy relationships based on mutual respect and understanding.

In conclusion, setting boundaries and asserting consent are essential components of healing and recovery for date rape survivors. By learning how to communicate their boundaries and assert their consent, survivors can protect themselves from harm, regain a sense of control over their bodies, and begin to rebuild their lives in a way that is empowering and fulfilling. It is important for women who have been drugged and suffered a date rape to know that they are not alone, and that there is help and support available to them as they navigate the healing process.

Redefining Relationships After Trauma

Recovery from a traumatic experience such as date rape involves not only healing physically and emotionally, but also reevaluating and redefining relationships in your life. For women who have been drugged and suffered a date rape, this can be an especially challenging process. It is important to recognize that the trauma you have experienced can have lasting effects on your ability to trust others and form healthy connections. However, it is possible to rebuild and redefine relationships in a way that is empowering and supportive.

Research into the consequences of date rape has shown that survivors often struggle with feelings of shame, guilt, and self-blame.

These negative emotions can impact the way survivors view themselves and others, making it difficult to establish healthy relationships.

It is essential for survivors to seek therapy or counseling to work through these emotions and develop a better understanding of how the trauma has affected their ability to connect with others. By addressing these underlying issues, survivors can begin to redefine their relationships in a more positive and fulfilling way.

Recovery and healing processes for date rape survivors often involve setting boundaries and communicating openly with others. It is important for survivors to assert their needs and desires in relationships, and to feel comfortable expressing their feelings and concerns. By establishing clear boundaries and practicing effective communication, survivors can create relationships that are based on mutual respect and understanding. This can help survivors feel more empowered and in control of their interactions with others, leading to healthier and more fulfilling relationships.

In redefining relationships after trauma, it is also important for survivors to surround themselves with a supportive network of friends, family, and professionals. Building a strong support system can provide survivors with the emotional and practical assistance they need to navigate the challenges of healing and recovery.

By seeking out individuals who are understanding, compassionate, and non-judgmental, survivors can create a safe and nurturing environment in which to explore their feelings and experiences. This support can help survivors feel less isolated and alone, and can encourage them to take positive steps towards rebuilding their lives.

Ultimately, redefining relationships after trauma is a deeply personal and individual process. Every survivor will have their own unique journey towards healing and recovery, and it is important to approach this process with patience, self-compassion, and an open mind.

By seeking out therapy, setting boundaries, communicating effectively, and building a strong support network, survivors can begin to redefine their relationships in a way that honors their experiences and empowers them to move forward with confidence and resilience. Healing from date rape is a challenging and complex process, but with the right tools and resources, survivors can begin to rebuild their lives and create relationships that are based on trust, respect, and mutual understanding.

Thriving Beyond Survival

In the subchapter "Thriving Beyond Survival," we will explore the journey of healing and recovery for women who have been drugged and suffered a date rape. While the experience of date rape can be incredibly traumatic and overwhelming, it is possible to move beyond mere survival and thrive in the aftermath. This section will focus on the importance of self-care, seeking support, and finding ways to reclaim power and agency in the face of such a violation.

Research into the consequences of date rape has shown that survivors often experience a range of physical, emotional, and psychological effects in the aftermath of the assault. These can include feelings of shame, guilt, fear, and confusion, as well as physical injuries and sexually transmitted infections. It is crucial for survivors to understand that these reactions are normal and valid, and that there is help available to support them through the healing process.

Recovery and healing processes for date rape survivors can be complex and challenging, but they are also incredibly empowering. By seeking therapy, joining support groups, and engaging in self-care practices such as meditation, exercise, and journaling, survivors can begin to process their trauma and rebuild their sense of self. It is important for survivors to remember that healing is a journey, and that it is okay to take things one step at a time.

One of the key aspects of thriving beyond survival is finding ways to reclaim power and agency in the aftermath of a date rape. This can involve setting boundaries with others, practicing self-compassion, and engaging in activities that bring joy and fulfillment. By taking back control over their lives and their bodies, survivors can begin to rebuild their sense of self-worth and confidence.

Ultimately, thriving beyond survival is about reclaiming one's sense of self and finding ways to live a fulfilling and meaningful life in spite of the trauma of date rape. By seeking support, engaging in self-care practices, and finding ways to reclaim power and agency, survivors can begin to heal and move forward in their recovery journey. Remember, you are not alone, and there is hope for a brighter future beyond the darkness of date rape.

Observe your thoughts.

Don't believe them.

They are not always true!!

- Eckhart Tolle

Chapter 13: Resources for Date Rape Survivors

Hotlines and Support Groups

Hotlines and support groups can be vital resources for women who have been drugged and suffered a date rape. These organizations provide a safe space for survivors to share their experiences, seek guidance, and connect with others who have gone through similar traumas. By reaching out to these hotlines and support groups, survivors can access the help and support they need to begin the healing and recovery process.

Research into the consequences of date rape has shown that survivors often experience a range of physical, emotional, and psychological effects in the aftermath of their assault.

These effects can include anxiety, depression, post-traumatic stress disorder, and substance abuse. By connecting with hotlines and support groups, survivors can access resources and information that can help them better understand and cope with these consequences.

In addition to providing emotional support, hotlines and support groups can also offer practical assistance to survivors of date rape. This can include information on reporting the assault to the authorities, accessing medical care, and seeking counseling services. By connecting with these organizations, survivors can receive guidance on navigating the complex aftermath of a date rape and taking steps towards healing and recovery.

Recovery and healing processes for date rape survivors can be long and challenging, but with the support of hotlines and support groups, survivors can begin to rebuild their lives and regain a sense of control and empowerment. By connecting with others who have experienced similar traumas, survivors can find validation, understanding, and a sense of community that can be invaluable in the healing process.

Overall, hotlines and support groups play a crucial role in providing support, resources, and guidance to women who have been drugged and suffered a date rape. By reaching out to these organizations, survivors can access the help they need to navigate the aftermath of their assault, begin the healing process, and reclaim their sense of self and agency.

Legal Rights and Options

In the aftermath of a traumatic experience like date rape, it is important for survivors to be aware of their legal rights and options. One of the first steps you can take is to report the assault to the police. It is crucial to document as much information as possible, including any evidence such as clothing, texts, or emails. You have the right to seek justice and hold the perpetrator accountable for their actions.

Seeking legal assistance is another important step in the process of healing and recovery. A lawyer who specializes in sexual assault cases can help you navigate the legal system and advocate for your rights. They can also provide guidance on filing a civil lawsuit against the perpetrator for damages such as medical expenses, therapy costs, and pain and suffering.

It is important to know that you are not alone in this journey. There are organizations and support groups that can provide you with the resources and support you need during this difficult time. These groups can offer counseling, therapy, and other services to help you heal from the trauma of date rape.

In addition to seeking legal assistance, it is important to prioritize your own self-care and well-being. This may include seeking therapy, practicing self-care activities such as yoga or meditation, and surrounding yourself with supportive friends and family members. It is normal to experience a range of emotions after a traumatic experience like date rape, and it is important to give yourself grace and time to heal.

Remember, you are a survivor, not a victim. You have the strength and resilience to overcome this trauma and move forward with your life. By seeking legal assistance, accessing support services, and prioritizing your own healing and recovery, you can begin to reclaim your power and find healing and peace after date rape.

Recommended Reading and Additional Support

For women who have been drugged and suffered a date rape, it is important to seek out additional resources and support to aid in the recovery and healing process. There are a number of books that can provide valuable insight and guidance for survivors of date rape. One such book is "The Courage to Heal: A Guide for Women Survivors of Child Sexual Abuse" by Ellen Bass and Laura Davis. This book offers practical advice on how to cope with the emotional aftermath of sexual trauma and provides tools for healing and recovery.

Another recommended reading for date rape survivors is "It Wasn't Your Fault: Freeing Yourself from the Shame of Childhood Abuse with the Power of Self-Compassion" by Beverly Engel. This book explores the impact of shame and self-blame on survivors of abuse and offers strategies for building self-compassion and self-esteem. By reading books like these, survivors can gain a better understanding of their experiences and learn how to navigate the challenges of healing and recovery.

In addition to reading books, survivors of date rape may benefit from seeking out additional support through therapy or support groups. Therapy can provide a safe space for survivors to process their experiences, work through trauma, and develop coping strategies. Support groups offer the opportunity to connect with others who have shared similar experiences and provide a sense of community and understanding.

For survivors interested in delving deeper into the research surrounding the consequences of date rape, there are a number of academic journals and articles that explore topics such as trauma, PTSD, and recovery. By staying informed about the latest research in this field, survivors can gain a better understanding of the long-term effects of date rape and the most effective strategies for healing and recovery.

Overall, seeking out recommended reading and additional support can be a valuable part of the healing and recovery process for date rape survivors. By educating themselves, connecting with others, and seeking professional help, survivors can empower themselves to heal and move forward from their traumatic experiences. Remember, you are not alone, and there is help available to support you on your journey towards healing and recovery.

Chapter 14: Prognose

How to proceed

The outlook is good. Through therapy, she can work through the trauma and find a way to cope with it.

Today, when I saw her again, my breath was taken away by her beauty. Her wavy groomed long hair cascaded down her back, adorned with a stunning deep red diadem. Her lips, painted with the same deep red hue, matched perfectly. Her eyes sparkled with brightness, enhanced by the careful application of makeup. Overwhelmed by her beauty, I couldn't help but offer her a heartfelt compliment, expressing how amazingly beautiful she looked.

Today we worked on her anger. Somehow, she cannot be angry. This anger was like a stone on her throat, belly and feet.

Remarkably, this anger is much older than the trauma... So there is still plenty to do, but she is willing to work on this because she feels the progress.

And this empowers her... That's precisely the goal. I utilize it to reinforce the positive emotions and resilience that arise from this. We explore her beliefs about anger in this session, and I believe she will emerge from it stronger.

Writing is a form of therapy; sometimes I wonder how all those who do not write,

compose or paint can manage to escape the madness,

the melancholia, the panic fear which is inherent in the human condition.

- Graham Greene

Chapter 15: Conclusion

Therapy helps!

Many of the symptoms can be linked to the cause, which is trauma. It does not matter whether client has memories of it or not. The impact, the consequences of the trauma on the brain and the consequences resulting from it, are, in my opinion, the same as a trauma of which a client does have memories.

The interventions focus on brain repair, stabilisation and increasing self-strength, self-strength and self-assurance. Again, the interventions are almost similar to the treatment of trauma with memories. Difference is in the use of memory. Here, I do not think it is helpful to force or want to use memories (too early) for an intervention such as regression or something similar. By doing so, I think you can actually worsen the client's condition in the beginning.

I haven't tested this, by the way, and it doesn't feel wise to me to do so. Now that the memories come up naturally, I can work with them.

My approach is based on giving back power and strength. Therefore, I find it appropriate to adapt the interventions accordingly and follow the client in this. In my opinion, this is the first step towards healing and letting her experience that she is in control of her own process.

There is only one path to happiness and that is to stop worrying about things you have no control over.

- Epictetus

EPILOGUE

Making small steps is still making progress!

We are now a few weeks into our sessions and I can report that we are still making progress together. Client was able to experience much more anger after the session on anger. It feels weird and uncomfortable for her because it is new to her.

I let her talk about her experiences and give her compliments for the work she has done. And that feeling anger is also a good thing. She fills it in herself "Because now I'm going to feel something..." How beautiful is that! She would like to look at this further today.

With some deepening questions, we get closer and closer to the core and eventually she gets to see where the anger (or rather, not being able to express anger) comes from. Now that the anger has found a place, and she can understand it, there is room for sadness. And today she walks out the door with a sense of sadness...

And while this too is beautiful, I can see that the grief is a logical consequence in her coping process. Even though this grief is not at all about the trauma of the date-rape, it is a step in her process of healing herself.

So that, little by little, she may feel herself whole and complete again. The cause, the memories or the lack of memories, that doesn't matter much, right now. We work on what is and on what can be. For this moment. And that's totally ok.

After reading, do you feel the need for personal contact? Do you still have questions or want to talk about this? Or do you have a tip? Then send me a message. I'd love to hear from you!

Special thanks

My sincere thanks goes to my client and respondents to my research for the trust they gave me and the courage they showed in sharing their stories with me.

Special thanks to Harold de Ruiter and Nancy de Ruiter-Flokstra for reading and editing. For giving me feedback and urging me to make it even better.

Special thanks to my children, they are my driving force to keep improving the world and myself.

And special thanks to my husband, my supporter, my rock. He brings out the best in me and what's more, he makes me feel like I can take on the whole world. Without him, this would never have become a reality.

With love,
Marga Hogenhuis

About the author

Marga Hogenhuis-Flokstra has completed a broad coaching education and an Integrative Psychoterapy course in which the following techniques were covered: Hypnotherapy, Rational Emotive Therapy (RET), ACT, Gestalt Therapy, modern short-term Psychodynamic therapies, Behavioural Therapy, Inner Child work, psychosomatics, Solution-Focused Therapy, Transactional Analysis (TA), Neuro-Linguistic Programming (NLP), Body-Oriented therapies, working with dreams, visualisations, working with sharing, Regression and coaching.

She also completed the Psychosocial and Medical Basic Knowledge training and developed a basic knowledge in the field of (developmental) psychology and psychopathology.

She has her own practice in Amsterdam, The Netherlands

Bibliography

A. Kardiner, A. S. (1947). War, Stress and Neurotic Illness. In A.

K. Spiegel. New York.

Claire, S., & Novak, W. (1997). Hart en ziel, de wonderbaarlijke gevolgen van een harttransplantatie. In S. Claire, & W. Novak, Hart en ziel, de wonderbaarlijke gevolgen van een harttransplantatie.

Derks, L. (2002). Sociale denkpatronen, NLP en het veranderen van onbewust sociaal gedrag. In L. Derks, Sociale denk- patronen, NLP en het veranderen van onbewust sociaal gedrag. Utrecht: Kosmos.

E. Stark, A. F. (1988). In A. F. E. Stark, Personal Power and Insi- tutional Victimization: Treating the dual Trauma of Woman Battering. New York.

GABA. (sd). Opgehaald van Ortho Health Foundation: https:// www.sohf.nl/nutrient/gaba

gevolgen-per-hersendeel/hypofyse. (sd). Opgehaald van www.hersenletsel-uitleg.nl: https://www.hersenletsel-uit-leg.nl/gevolgen/gevolgen-per-hersendeel/hypofyse

gevolgen-per-hersendeel/hypothalamus. (sd). Opgehaald van www.hersenletsel-uitleg.nl: https://www.hersenletsel-uit-leg.nl/gevolgen/gevolgen-per-hersendeel/hypothalamus

Herman, J. (2016). Trauma & Herstel. In J. Herman, Trauma & Herstel.

https://www.hersendeel/amygdala. (sd). Opgehaald van https:// www.hersenletsel-uitleg.nl/: https://www.hersenletsel-uitleg.nl/gevolgen/gevolgen-per-hersendeel/amygdala

https://www.hersenletsel-uitleg.nl/gevolgen/gevolgen-per-her-sendeel/hippocampus. (sd). Opgehaald van www.hersen- letsel-uitleg.nl: https://www.hersenletsel-uitleg.nl/gevol-gen/gevolgen-per-hersendeel/hippocampus

https://www.jellinek.nl/vraag-antwoord/wat-is-rohypnol/. (sd).

Opgehaald van https://www.jellinek.nl/vraag-ant-woord/wat-is-rohypnol/: Bron: https://www.jellinek.nl/vraag-antwoord/wat-is-rohypnol/

is-ghb-een-verkrachtingsdrug-of-een-date-rape-drug/.
(sd). Op- gehaald van www.jellinek.nl:
https://www.jellinek.nl/ vraag-antwoord/is-ghb-een-
verkrachtingsdrug-of-een- date-rape-drug/

Korf, J. e. (2002). GHB tussen Extase en Narcose. Korf,
J. e.a.

GHB tussen Extase en Narcose (2002).

Nemeth. (2010). The involvement of GHB in reported
sexual assaults. Journal of psychopharmacology.

neurotransmitters. (sd). Opgehaald van
deelbewust.com: http://
deelbewust.com/neurotransmitters

Olgers, J. (2005). Handboek Hypnotherapie. Heelheid
in wor- ding: De praktijk van hypnose- en
regressietherapie. In J. Olgers, Handboek
Hypnotherapie. Heelheid in wording: De praktijk van
hypnose- en regressietherapie. Houten: Zwerk
Uitgevers.

Pearsall, P. (1998). Het geheugen van het hart,
Onverwachte ge- volgen van harttransplantaites. . In
P. Pearsall, Het ge- heugen van het hart,
Onverwachte gevolgen van hart- transplantaites. .

Symonds, M. (1982). Victom Responses to Terror: Understan- ding and Treatment. In M. Symonds. Boulder.

www.brainclinics.com/depressie. (sd). Opgehaald van www.- brainclinics.com: https://www.brainclinics.com/depres- sie

www.jellinek.nl. (sd). Opgehaald van https://www.jellinek.nl/ vraag-antwoord/is-ghb-een-verkrachtingsdrug-of-een- date-rape-drug/: https://www.jellinek.nl/vraag-ant- woord/is-ghb-een-verkrachtingsdrug-of-een-date-rape- drug

Breaking the Silence

What lies before you is a personal study on the consequences of a date-rape. In this research, I sought answers to the following questions: What are the psychological and (psycho)somatic symptoms associated with this particular trauma? What interventions can I apply? How can I help the best way possible? As a therapist, how do you deal with the fact that there are virtually no memories? The book provides answers to these questions and gives an overview of possible interventions. I hope this is a step in the direction of greater awareness and openness so that this comes out of the taboo sphere.

Other titles from this author:
- Using writing as therapy:
Workbook 10 steps on how to utilize writing as a form of therapy.

-Rational Emotive Therapy:
Workbook RET in 7 steps.

www.MargaHogenhuis.nl